The best Gluten Free Recipes

For Beginners

Author

Randi B. Carty

Understanding Gluten (Chapter 1)

This chapter will teach you everything you need to know about gluten and how to avoid it. People will be curious about gluten once they learn you are gluten-free, and they will ask you questions about it. You'll be the authority!

What Exactly Is Gluten?

Let's start with the definition of gluten from Webster's Dictionary:

"A strong, elastic protein substance, particularly wheat flour, that gives dough its cohesion."

See the Concise Encyclopedia for a more detailed explanation: Wheat and other cereal grains contain a mixture of proteins that are not easily soluble in water. Gluten is present in flour, and its presence allows leavened baked goods to be made. Gluten molecules form a flexible network that traps carbon dioxide and expands along with it. Gluten has different properties depending on where it comes from. Doughs can be soft, extensible, or tough and elastic, depending on the gluten content in the flours.

However, these definitions leave out crucial information about gluten-free eating.

Gluten is a protein found in wheat, rye, and other cereal grains. It is, however, found in dough and other wheat products. The medical community's common definition of gluten, as I use it throughout the book, is:

"A protein blend made primarily of wheat, barley, and rye."

This definition is much broader, and it includes other grains that should be avoided when eating gluten-free. Gluten from wheat, barley, and rye can be used in a variety of ways other than baking.

Gluten-free people do not have to consume the entire meal. Gluten from corn and rice differs from gluten from wheat, barley, or rye in that their protein structures are different. Corn and rice are used to make many gluten-free products.

What is the Function of Gluten?

Gluten is a healthy ingredient that can be found in a wide variety of foods and products. Gluten... Enhances elasticity

Is there a filler?

Is there a thickener? Is a flavor enhancer and adds protein Is a binder necessary?

Gluten is a fantastic ingredient for a variety of reasons.

There are a few gluten-containing foods that are surprising (because they aren't made from dough):

Dressing for salad Seasonings/spice blends for soup Soy sauce with licorice

Along with food, gluten can be found in cosmetics, shampoos, and flavored beverages. Gluten can be found in a variety of foods. When you first start this diet, almost everything appears to contain gluten!

But don't be alarmed! There's still hope! There are many gluten-free foods and products available, all of which are manufactured by reputable companies (which I will discuss in the next chapters).

I want you to understand why gluten can cause problems for some people before I get into the world of gluten-free food.

What exactly is the issue with gluten?

You now have a better understanding of gluten and how to use it. What exactly is the issue with gluten?

Gluten can cause negative reactions in people with celiac disease, autoimmune disease, or those who are gluten sensitive.

Gluten could be to blame for this reaction. The medical community has yet to find an answer to this question, and there are numerous theories. It is clear, however, that reactions do occur and that the causes are not as "in your head" as some doctors and health professionals once believed (and unfortunately still do).

Gluten sensitivities are real, and they can manifest themselves in a variety of ways. Some people get indigestion, while others develop a skin reaction to gluten. Celiac disease affects some people. Gluten sensitivities come in a variety of forms, each of which can cause a variety of health issues.

Gluten intolerance is another term for non-celiac gluten intolerance. Despite the fact that gluten intolerance is not an auto-immune disorder like celiac or celiac disease, the symptoms can be very similar. Gluten sensitivity can cause digestive issues or allergic reactions. Gas and diarrhea are two common symptoms, as are lethargy and fogginess. Rashes, headaches, and nasal congestion are also possible side effects. When gluten is removed from your diet or applied to products, these symptoms go away.

Another possibility is celiac disease. Celiac disease is an auto-immune disorder caused by gluten sensitivity. Gluten is a problem for celiac disease sufferers. Gluten triggers an immune response because the body perceives it as something it should fight.

What is Celiac Disease and How Does It Affect You?

Celiac disease is the most common autoimmune disorder, affecting both children and adults. Celiac disease affects about one in every 100 adults. Even more people are at risk if they have the symptoms.

Gluten damages the small villi, which are nutrient-absorbing threads that look like hair. They are found in the small intestine's upper portion. When gluten comes into contact with villi, the body perceives it as an invasion. When the immune system attacks gluten, the villi are damaged. If the villi become flattened, the body is unable to absorb nutrients from food.

Conditions like osteoporosis and infertility can develop if you don't eat well.

How does celiac disease manifest itself? People with certain genetic characteristics are more likely to develop celiac disease. They may be born with the disease, even if they do not have a genetic predisposition to it. Even if you don't have the genes, you can be diagnosed.

Celiac disease symptoms and related symptoms can strike anyone at any time. Others may not experience any symptoms or be able to recognize the problem for years. Unknown triggers can cause the disease suddenly and without warning, and they aren't always consistent.

Celiac disease does not imply that you are allergic to gluten or that you are gluten intolerant. Celiac disease is not caused by a virus or a cold. Once celiac disease has become active, it can be fatal. Gluten sensitivities in other forms can also go away.

What are the symptoms of celiac disease or gluten sensitivity? You can find out by having your blood tested. You can also tell if you're having the usual symptoms. The symptoms are classified as silent, atypical, or classical by the medical community.

What are the Celiac Disease Symptoms?

Celiac disease or gluten sensitivity can manifest itself in a variety of ways. To make matters more difficult, each individual is different and may have their own set of signs.

Are you a celiac disease candidate? If you or a member of your family is experiencing symptoms that are similar to those listed below, you should consult your doctor.

It's critical to get a celiac diagnosis before beginning a gluten-free diet. If you eat gluten-free, doctors will be unable to diagnose you.

In addition to the appearance of the villi in the small intestine, standardized tests can detect the body's reaction to gluten in blood work. If you have a gluten sensitivity, your body will begin to heal as soon as you stop eating gluten-free. This makes it more difficult to diagnose your condition.

The classic symptoms of illness differ depending on whether the patient is a child, a young adult, or an adult. (Please keep in mind that I am not a physician.) These are the results of a compilation process. information gleaned from books, the Internet, and my own experience

SYMPTOMS OF A CHILDREN

Diarrhea

Large, distended belly due to stunted growth or "failure to thrive," as some doctors refer to it

It appears that a child is hungry or malnourished.

After meals, you vomit Appetite slowed

Is it difficult for you to gain or lose weight?

Irritability Constipation fatigue

Gluten sensitivity can cause a variety of symptoms in infants and children. It's clear if they're not getting enough nutrition.

These symptoms reminded me of my celiac-disease-affected daughter. After all these years, it's still difficult to persuade doctors to order celiac disorder tests, but that's slowly changing. If your doctor isn't interested in gluten and isn't knowledgeable about it, find another doctor. Don't give up if you notice these symptoms in your child. If you discover what's going on sooner, your child's health will improve.

SYMPTOMS OF AN ADULT

Diarrhea Growth stifled The pain in your stomach Gassy

Fatigue as a result of weight loss or being underweight Irritability

Depression Skin rash that persists

FOR ADULTS SYMPTOMS

Insomnia Osteoporosis Depression achy joints Arthritis

diarrhea that lasts for a long time

SYMPTOMS THAT ARE COMMON AND SILENT

A lack of iron Anemia problems with the gallbladder Dermatitis herpetiformis is a chronic skin rash. Deficiency in the B vitamin folic acid

Infertility that has no known cause

Multiple symptoms can appear in adults. Adults with celiac disease can be asymptomatic for a long time until secondary diseases such as diabetes reveal the presence of celiac disease.

The above symptoms could affect you, your child, or a family member. To rule out celiac disease, you should speak with a doctor.

A gluten-free diet can help people with Celiac disease and its symptoms. It's comforting to know that a simple dietary change may be beneficial. No surgery or medication is required.

All you have to do is eat wisely and healthily.

What treatments are available for Celiac Disease and Gluten Intolerance?

You must stop eating gluten to be gluten-free completely. Period!

It can take weeks or months to get back to feeling normal. It could take months or even years for people who have had celiac disease for some time. After a few days, many celiacs and gluten intolerant people feel better. It is possible that it will occur very quickly!

Summary

Gluten is a microscopic protein found in wheat, barley, and rye, and you learned about it in this chapter.

Gluten can cause unpleasant reactions in people who are allergic to it, as you learned. Celiac disease is the world's most common autoimmune disorder, and those who have it must follow a gluten-free diet for the rest of their lives.

Gluten sensitivity and celiac disease have a wide range of symptoms that vary from person to person. As a result, before starting a gluten-free diet, you should get tested for celiac disease if you have any symptoms. A gluten-free diet is the most effective strategy to treat gluten sensitivity and celiac disease.

Eating gluten-free isn't easy. Is this something you can do? It's possible to eat gluten-free with a proper strategy.

Prepare to Eat Gluten-Free in Chapter 2

The first few weeks are the most challenging of a gluten-free diet. It's tough to know where to eat and what to eat at first, particularly in the first few weeks. You may feel lost while contemplating a lifestyle shift. However, by preparing ahead and being dedicated, you may overcome your sense of loss.

This section will show you how to eat gluten-free with confidence. You'll figure out how to keep track of your progress and make a weekly eating plan. Additionally, I demonstrate how to make a shopping list.

How to Keep Tabs on Your Development

There is a wealth of gluten-free information accessible. What system do you use to keep track of everything? Keeping track of all critical information and your progress can help you avoid being overwhelmed.

Your diary is an excellent resource for keeping note of any advice from your doctor. As you make the shift to gluten-free diet, it might help you evaluate what's working well and where you might need support.

Here are some ideas for diary entries: Foods you like that are gluten-free

Have any questions? Dinner suggestions

When you first became ill, what you ate, and when you first became ill

before

How you're feeling now that you've started eating gluten-free

A journal may be made using a three-ring binder, folders, and paper. Handouts, magazine clippings, and Internet printouts, as well as any other material you may have, may all be stored in the folders. You may create notes and monitor your progress on the paper.

Make a list of all of your favorite recipes and items. Make a list of any errors you encounter (and you will).

Observe your signs and symptoms. Keep note of which meals appear to benefit you and which should be avoided. The reactions of your body will offer you hints. You may measure your progress and shorten your learning curve by keeping note of your triumphs and mistakes.

Recipes, Notes, and Products may all be organized in your binder. This will make organizing and accessing your information much simpler. This is a private diary of yours.

It's possible to make and utilize an electronic journal. With apps like these, Evernote makes taking notes a breeze. Evernote enables you to use your smartphone to snap photographs of recipes, download pages from the Internet, and arrange all of this material into folders that can subsequently be shared across your phone, tablet, and PC.

It's time to plan what you'll eat for the first week after you've established a system for measuring how your gluten-free diet is going. Planning ahead is an excellent practice even if you don't eat gluten-free.

What You Should Do First

This section includes seven days' worth of meal and snack ideas. It also contains advice on how to handle typical issues.

The first week of adopting gluten-free foods and cooking should be your priority. Knowing what you'll eat each day might be challenging.

Breakfast, lunch, and supper ideas are included in this one-week meal plan. Five of the seven breakfasts are ideal for a hectic day at the office. You can make all of these dishes at home. Until you have more experience cooking gluten-free, these dishes are simple to make. All ingredients must be gluten-free: this is a given.

Meal Planning for a Week

This book's recipes may be found at the back. Then choose "Recipes" from the Table of Contents.

Breakfast

Fresh fruit and yogurt

Chex cereal (excluding Wheat Chex) and fruit from General Mills - look for "gluten-free" on the top of the package.

Sausage with scrambled eggs sliced red pepper, poached egg

(A well-known brand is Udi's) Bagel a cream cheese mixture Fruit salad, pancakes, scrambled eggs tacos de maana

Lunch

a sarnie (gluten-free bread, Hormel Natural Selections packaged deli meat, sliced cheese) Quesadilla made out of corn tortillas

Salad Chef

Annie's Tomato Soup with Grilled Cheese Sandwich is one example.

Fruit with a protein shake (for example, Arbonne's protein mix) Nachos Steamed veggies with baked potato

Dinner

Burger with fries and tacos Salad

a sauce for pasta

Broccoli and beef stir-fry

Enchiladas de pollo with pollo de pollo de pollo de pollo de pollo de pollo de pollo Pork with a sour and sweet flavor

Snacks

carrots (baby)

Potato Chips, Lay's Original Doritos with Cool Ranch Rolls Tootsie

Peanut Multi-Grain M&M's Crunchmaster Crackers Fruit Roll-Ups, Betty Crocker

Cinnamon Apple Sauce from Musselman's

Cashews Frito-Lay

Over the course of seven days, there are 21 meals available. You may also combine the meals to create daily meals.

Then, depending on your meal planning, make a shopping list.

What is a Grocery List and How Do You Make One?

Offering gluten-free items to consumers is getting increasingly common, but finding appetizing meals may still be tough. Finding the correct food is simpler with a shopping list.

If your store doesn't have the product you want, seek for gluten-free substitutes and add them to your shopping list. The shopping list for the One Week Meal Plan may be seen in the example below. (I provide several gluten-free choices in the chapter "Be Confident"):

Produce

lettuce (head) Greens in a mixture Onion Tomato Garlic peppers (bell) Potatoes

Fruit that is still in season (whatever is in season that you like)

Meat

Beef patty Chops de porc Breasts of chicken Stir-fried beef

Meat for lunch (Hormel Natural Selections and Oscar Mayer).

Dairy

Cheddar is a type of cheese.

Monterey Cheesy Jack (Kraft and Tillamook). Eggs

yogurt with sour cream (Frigo, Tillamook)

Yogurt is a delicious dairy product (Stonyfield Yoplait, Yoplait if gluten-free).

Miscellaneous

Cereal (Cinnamon, chocolate, honey nut, rice, corn, General Mills Chex) Shells for tacos (Ortega) tortillas made of corn (Mission, Ortega)

Chips made from tortillas (On The Border, Tostitos). Pasta is a type of pasta that is made (Tinkyada, DeBoles)

Depending on where you live, gluten-free products may be difficult to come by. However, you can order food online and have it delivered to your home, so this should not be an issue. These websites sell gluten-free goods for a reasonable price:

Amazon.com: Amazon Prime members receive free two-day shipping and free overnight shipping.

One of the first online gluten-free supermarkets is Celiac.com – The Gluten-Free Mall.

Summary

Keep a journal where you can jot down questions, useful hints, gluten-free recipes, and research materials, as well as organize printouts, recipes, and research materials.

Plan your meals ahead of time to make shopping and eating gluten-free easier.

Make a grocery list that includes gluten-free brands so you know what to buy.

Maintaining a gluten-free diet can be difficult. However, don't think in terms of months or weeks. Take each day as it comes. Baby steps, baby steps, baby steps...

If you eat gluten-containing food by accident, you can correct your symptoms and work on feeling better. A gluten-free diet will become second nature to you, and it will become an integral part of your healthier lifestyle.

Be Aware of Cross-Contamination in Chapter 3

It can be as simple as a few crumbs from the wrong foods to make you sick. Gluten cross-contamination is a problem because even a small amount can cause serious issues.

When gluten-free foods are in close proximity to gluten-containing foods, cross-contamination occurs. Cross-contamination can occur in a variety of settings, such as restaurants, condiment jars, and even your kitchen counter.

How can you keep your gluten-free food safe from cross-contamination? Crosscontamination is something that can be understood, as well as where and how it happens and how to avoid it.

Cross-Contamination is a term used to describe when two or more people come into contact with each other.

When gluten-containing food (such as breadcrumbs) is mixed with gluten-free food, this is referred to as cross-contamination. When gluten-free foods are cooked in the same appliances or cookware as gluten-containing foods, crosscontamination can occur.

Gluten is a living organism, despite its microscopic size. Gluten intolerance and celiac disease patients must consume it to have a reaction. Some people are so sensitive to gluten that even ingesting flour dust or applying gluten-containing lotions to their skin can cause them to react.

Gluten-sensitive people can have an allergic reaction even if they eat crouton crumbs.

The best way to avoid inhaling gluten is to avoid cross-contamination. Because different foods are frequently fried in the same oil, a deep fryer is an obvious example. Is it possible for gluten-free foods to become contaminated?

Cross-Contamination Can Happen Anywhere

Cross-contamination can occur in your own home, at a friend's house, or at a restaurant. Food is prepared and consumed anywhere.

The most common places for this to happen are kitchen countertops, griddles, and grills. It can also happen when bread crumbs fall into butter, mayonnaise, or a jelly container from utensils.

When wheat flour dust and vegetables are left on the same cutting board, cross-contamination occurs.

A pasta strainer is another issue. Even if your gluten-free pasta is cooked separately, it could be placed in a contaminated container (washing it in cold water won't remove all cross-contamination).

Perhaps you're anticipating a summer barbecue. Chicken or burgers cooked on the same grill as buns can make you sick if you're gluten intolerant. Cross-contamination is a risk in restaurants that cook a variety of foods on grills.

A salad containing croutons can still be contaminated even if all of the croutons have been removed.

Your gluten-free meal can contain gluten in a variety of ways, causing you to become ill. You must still eat and go about your daily routine. So, how do you ensure the safety of your food?

How can you ensure the safety of your food at home?

You are in command of your kitchen. You have complete control over the storage, cleaning, and cooking of your food. This should make gluten-free cooking a breeze. Cross-contamination can be avoided in the following ways:

Ensure that all cooking surfaces are clean, with no crumbs, flour dust, or other potentially harmful by-products left on the counters.

Ensure that all pots, pans, and cooking utensils are clean.

Using gluten-free cutting boards and pasta strainers is a must. They must never be used for anything else.

Label your containers boldly to keep your food safe. Keep gluten-free foods sealed and away from gluten-containing foods.

Even if they don't have gluten issues, make sure everyone in your household knows how to handle the food, cookware, and post-cooking cleanup. Other family members may become ill as a result of their indifference.

These are the most important considerations when preparing your kitchen for gluten-free cooking.

How do you know your food is safe when you're not at home?

Outside of your home, cross-contamination can be more difficult. In a restaurant, it's difficult to see the kitchen. Although you are aware that someone is preparing your food, it is impossible to observe the process. It's possible that fries are fried alongside other foods in the same fryer. I don't eat them, or any other food that might be prepared in a fryer, because it's too dangerous.

If you don't have access to the kitchen or those who prepare your food, how can you avoid cross-contamination? Inquire about the food's preparation with the wait staff. Ask! You're paying for the meal; it's not the restaurant's responsibility to ensure that you eat safely!

Pose questions from various angles, such as: You:

Is it true that your fries are gluten-free?

Is the fryer used for anything else? What can I do to ensure that my food is not contaminated by gluten?

What steps does your restaurant take to ensure that its food is gluten-free?

How do you keep gluten from cross-contaminating your food in the kitchen?

I'm asking these questions because I'm gluten-intolerant and don't want to throw up at the dinner table.

Waiter: I'll inquire with the chef.

Following up with more questions can help you gain clarity. Although there are no guarantees, wait staff and chefs' willingness to answer your questions demonstrates that they care.

You can ask these questions to your family and friends. You don't want them to cook something that makes you sick. Inquire about the food's ingredients, where it was purchased (organic or regular supermarket), and how it was prepared.

Make sure they understand how important it is for them to be able to prepare a healthy meal for you. The dangers of gluten and celiac disease are becoming more widely recognized.

To cross-contaminate a gluten-free meal, all it takes is a crumb or two. Contamination can occur in restaurants as well as in your own home kitchen.

By sanitizing cooking surfaces and using gluten-free cookware, you can protect the food you prepare in your kitchen. To avoid accidental use, make sure all gluten-free food containers or packages are clearly labeled.

You can protect yourself by inquiring about the preparation of your food outside the home.

Gluten is found in a variety of foods. Be grateful to anyone who makes an effort to accommodate you, even if they fail occasionally. They'll be more likely to try again if you're cooking for them. Ask questions to gain a better understanding of how the food was prepared, and don't be afraid to seek clarification.

"If you don't know, don't eat it!" is a good motto to live by.

The best place to avoid cross-contamination is in your kitchen. How can you make sure your kitchen is safe for gluten-free cooking and eating? This is the next section of the book.

GF At Home (Chapter 4)

You should be able to prepare and eat gluten-free meals in a secure environment. What steps can you take to make this happen? Follow this step-by-step guide to ensure that you and your family live in a gluten-free, cross-contamination-free environment.

Before you can convert your refrigerator and pantry to gluten-free foods, you'll need a well-thought-out plan. To begin, determine whether the kitchen can be made completely gluten-free. This will be determined by how many members of your family are adopting the new diet.

You won't be the only one who makes this choice. Many people are doing it all over the country. Karen and I have heard of families who have eliminated gluten from their diets and made their kitchens gluten-free.

Are you already ridding your home of gluten?

When our daughter was diagnosed with celiac disease, my wife and I decided to go gluten-free. Seeing my daughter grow into a healthy young lady has been well worth the effort, even if it was difficult at times.

You won't have to be concerned about cross-contamination or food labeling. You must maintain a gluten-free environment in your home.

You can read the rest of this chapter even if you've already made your home gluten-free. When you travel, for example, you may find yourself cooking in someone else's kitchen. This article will help you avoid these situations.

In a shared kitchen, how do you keep food safe?

Sharing gluten-free items with other gluten-free foods is possible, but you'll need to take extra precautions to keep your gluten-free food safe. Nongluten items will need to be kept on a separate shelf in your pantry or refrigerator. Pantry

Keeping gluten-free foods in sealed containers is beneficial in several ways. It protects your gluten-free food from cross-contamination from food particles. The container is portable, allowing food to be transported from one location to another.

Stock your shelves with gluten-free items like crackers and flour once the space is ready. The containers can then be labeled with a permanent marker or large, legible labels to indicate what is inside.

Kitchen

In some cases, gluten-free and non-gluten products are available. When a utensil is used, cross-contamination can occur (e.g., to spread a condiment on a sandwich using a knife). If you're using the most common items in a shared kitchen, it's safer to have two sets. In your kitchen, you can have peanut butter, mustard, jam, and butter. Make sure they're gluten-free by labeling them as such.

You can keep gluten-free condiments, salad dressings, and perishable foods on your gluten-free shelves. A large label on the shelves that reads "Gluten Free" is a great idea to let others in the house know that the food is safe.

If you share a kitchen, you should have separate cookware. A pasta strainer, chopping board, and cookie sheets are all required. In your pantry, place them on the appropriate shelf.

For a group of people who cook together, brightly colored cookware and utensils are a good idea. Labels with a lot of color are also an option. This will alert everyone in your home to the presence of red labels on your gluten-free cookware. This is just one method for avoiding cross-contamination by accident.

Now that you know how to make your kitchen gluten-free, it's time to tell the rest of your family about your plans.

Sharing Your Strategy

Are you already planning how you'll make room in your kitchen for gluten-free foods? It's a good idea to let those who share your kitchen space in on your gluten-free cooking strategy.

Create a plan and share it with everyone to educate them. Knowing your strategy will reduce the chances of your family members inadvertently consuming your costly cookies or causing cross contamination.

Consider topics such as food labeling and storage. What should I do with the food that I have? Your gluten-free appliances, cookware, and utensils will be stored in this area. What method of preparation do you intend to use?

You can add any other information that is relevant to your specific situation as you become more comfortable with your new lifestyle.

Schedule a meeting with everyone in your household after you've finished your plan. If you go over the steps in detail, you might be able to get some good ideas and feedback from your family. Going gluten-free for the first time can be challenging.

I tend to talk mostly about my family because of my family's lifestyle. This guide is also useful for visitors and roommates, as well as anyone who will be dining in your home and needs to know about your personal situation.

Now is the time to put your strategy into action. Where do you begin, however? Following that, I'll provide you with gluten-free kitchen checklists.Kitchen Checklist for Shared Spaces

If you share your kitchen with others, this list will help you ensure that you have a safe space to cook and eat gluten-free food. These are some practical ideas for making more space in your kitchen. In your kitchen, you should make the most of every square inch!

Choose a shelf or drawer in the refrigerator as your personal space. Find a new location for the foods that are currently available. Clean the shelf or drawer thoroughly with a towel. Put a gluten-free label on this area now.

Choose a shelf in the pantry or cupboard to call your own. Find a new home for the items that are currently in that location. It should be thoroughly cleaned. Put a gluten-free label on this area now.

If your utensil drawer is near a place where others prepare gluten-containing foods, clean it out and make it a habit to do so on a regular basis.

Clean out your kitchen utensils drawer (if you have one) and plan to do so on a regular basis if it collects crumbs. Choose a set of food storage containers to use for leftovers.

Purchase a few cooking utensils, such as spoons and spatulas. It is not necessary to purchase a separate muffin pan, cookie sheet, or cutting board, but if you can afford it, it is the safest option. If you're going to share these items with gluten-containing foods, make sure they're extra clean before using them in gluten-free recipes.

Eventually, you'll need a toaster or toaster oven. If you buy some Toastabags, which are Teflon envelopes that protect your bread or bagel from touching any crumbs in the toaster, you can get away with sharing a toaster with everyone else. On Amazon.com, they are reasonably priced. Begin purchasing gluten-free foods.

Checklist for Dedicating Your Kitchen to Gluten-Free Cooking

If you live alone or with others who are going gluten-free, I recommend taking these precautions to keep your kitchen free of cross contamination.

1. Remove all foods containing wheat, barley, or rye from your diet.

2. Remove any potentially contaminated foods from the equation.

Condiments (such as ketchup, mustard, and mayonnaise), spreads (such as peanut butter), and jam jars, for example, may contain gluten crumbs.

3. Get rid of gluten-containing plastic food storage containers.

4. Discard any strainers, toaster, or other utensils or cookware that may have been contaminated. However, if you have a toaster oven, keep it because you can clean it and cook your food with aluminum foil.

5. Always, always, always, always, always, always, always, always, always, always, Scrub the pots, pans, and baking sheets, as well as the utensil drawer. Clean the fridge, pantry, and cabinets to ensure there are no crumbs. Clean cutting boards, especially those made of wood or plastic. Their surfaces may be absorbent, and residue from previous uses may be present. It has a pleasant

scent and is completely safe to use. It wouldn't hurt to wash the walls with water and baking soda after you've cleaned out the fridge. It sanitizes and deodorizes organically.

With new utensils and cookie sheets, a new toaster, and new food storage containers, you can start over. One of each item will suffice. You can still clean and sanitize existing storage containers, cookie sheets, and utensils if buying new isn't an option. Because there is no way to make the toaster gluten-free, it must be used.

Start stocking your pantry with gluten-free foods and you'll be fine.

Summary

Decide whether you'll have gluten-free and gluten-containing foods in your kitchen, or if you can make it completely gluten-free.

If you have to share your kitchen with gluten-free and gluten-free people (depending on who will be using the new meal plan), make sure everyone in the family is aware of your plans.

Ascertain that the food, cookware, pantry, refrigerator, and eating area are gluten-free. Sanitize the kitchen thoroughly, including the pantry and refrigerator.

To avoid cross-contamination, clearly label storage spaces and containers as gluten-free.

If you take these precautions to ensure that the foods you eat and the cookware you use are free of cross contamination, your body will heal completely. You'll feel fantastic and wonder why you didn't do this sooner!

How to Eat Gluten-Free at Parties (Chapter 5)

Is it difficult to believe you've been invited to a party? It would be fantastic to get to know everyone. Gluten, gluten, gluten! What can you eat without getting sick? The party loses its allure for you, and you consider declining the invitation.

Don't give up! Even if you don't eat gluten, you can still have a good time at the party. You don't have to give up having fun and socializing while adjusting to a gluten-free diet!

How to Get Ready for the Big Day

You should go to the party and drink and eat with the rest of the guests. You can still have fun at the party without having to worry about putting everything on a plate. However, before you go, you should do some research.

Find out as much as you can about the foods and beverages you'll be serving. Is there a selection of vegetable and cheese trays? Soda or juice, which do you prefer? Do you think the hostess would mind if you brought your own food or drink?

You might be able to guess what they're serving based on their invitation. If you have any doubts, please contact them and inform them. Despite your embarrassment, it is critical that you obtain additional information for your safety and health.

If the gathering is small and intimate, inquire about the food that will be served. If the party is being held in a restaurant or hotel, inquire ahead of time if gluten-free options are available. It may come as a surprise to learn that they have gluten-free options on their menus and that certain items can be customized to your preferences.

It's time to decide what to bring to the party after you've done your research.

What Should You Bring?

When you eat out, don't assume that there will be gluten-free options available. You should bring your own gluten-free snacks and beverages. My wife and I keep non-perishable food and beverages in our car. She keeps some in her purse as well. It allows me to attend last-minute events with greater ease.

If you follow the suggestions, you should have a good idea of what kind of food you'll be serving. After that, you must purchase or prepare food that meets your requirements. This includes fruits, vegetables, and cheeses, as well as a main course if the meal is served at a table. You can ask for a gluten-free substitute if the restaurant offers them.

It's possible that your kitchen already has a plan (e.g. Make gluten-free crackers or a vegetable dip as well. You can bring your favorite salsas, dressings, and corn chips or make your own.

Dessert is often served at parties, so you should be able to indulge in some sweet treats! Gluten-free brownies, cookies, and cupcakes are all possible. You can either make something from scratch or buy something from the store to bring to the party.

Gluten-free foods are always a good choice, such as:

Crackers and Chips Cupcakes with Salsa Dressing Brownies Cheese Cookies Salad with vegetables on a tray

Salad of fruits

You don't want your food to come into contact with anything that could contaminate it. Put your name and "glutenfree" on the containers.

You now have a better idea of what to bring to the party. If you're bringing your own food to the party, what should you do?

What to Expect When You Get There

You've come prepared to have a good time, but what about all the food you've brought? So, what exactly do you do? Begin by extending a warm welcome to the host and guests. Then proceed directly to the kitchen.

If you have enough space, you can store food in the refrigerator or on a counter. Get a plate to serve your food on if you don't have enough space. It makes no difference if you eat it right away. You're free to put it aside. If your food is mixed in with other food trays, there is a risk of cross-contamination. You don't want gluten to be exposed after all of your efforts to ensure that your food is safe. Don't go overboard. Your health should always come first.

At any dinner party, you can ask for gluten-free options. They'll almost certainly have more information. They can also provide you with answers to your questions.

Keep your ears and eyes peeled for anything unusual. Even if you don't have celiac disease or gluten sensitivity, you might meet someone with special dietary needs at the party. Inquire about their diet and the type of menu they follow. Education, education, education!

But hold on! What do you do with gluten-free food now that you know how to make it?

What Should You Drink?

After you've settled in and had a good time, you'll want to have a drink. Gluten-free beverages can be made in a variety of ways.

Water is safe, but tea is not. Did you know that some brands contain barley? I didn't know that barley was an ingredient in some brands. I assumed it was tea. Avoid it unless you are familiar with the ingredients. Coffee is fine, by the way.

Safe for many sodas, including Coke, Pepsi, and their diet varieties. As long as the juice is 100 percent , it's safe. Capri Sun is safe if children are present at the party.

Tonic water and wine are safe. Experts in the gluten-free community agree that vodka, whiskey, and tequila can be safely distilled because they are free of gluten.

Beer can contain hops and malt, barley, wheat grain, and/or both. There are many good gluten- free options available. If beer is your preferred drink, you can call liquor stores ahead to check what they have. BYOB is completely acceptable at most parties and barbecues.

Relax and have fun. Enjoy your time and enjoy the company of friends!

Summary

Preparing ahead is key to having fun at a party and remaining gluten-free. Get as much information about the food and drinks that will be served as possible.

Bring your own gluten-free pre-labeled food and beverages! Even a simple plate of crackers and cheese can make you feel physically more comfortable and less conspicuous. When you first arrive, find a safe place to keep your food. If the refrigerator is too crowded, serve yourself immediately to prevent crosscontamination.

Many beverages are gluten-free, including sodas like Coke and Pepsi, wine, vodka and whiskey. Juice is also a great option.

You don't have to be gluten-free in order to enjoy the food at parties. You can bring gluten-free snacks and food to parties. You'll learn more about what to bring and what to order at every event or party.

Social events have different expectations than dining at restaurants. Similar obstacles can arise when you eat out or go to a party. I will discuss this in the next chapter.

Chapter 6: Eating Gluten-Free at Restaurants

You can eat at restaurants and get away from your home to enjoy great food and meet new people. It's also great because there is no need to cook or prepare dishes.

Is it possible to eat out while eating gluten-free?

Is it safe to eat at restaurants?

It is possible to eat in restaurants safely. However, dining out comes with certain risks.

Restaurant kitchens are bustling with activity. Many dishes can be prepared simultaneously. Staff and chefs are often busy cooking meals in shared workspaces. This creates the possibility of cross-contamination. Bread crumbs can accidentally get lost in the chaos of making salads. What you thought would be a delicious gluten-free salad turns out to be an unpleasant surprise.

Your food will be handled by different people. A waiter will take your order, while a chef will prepare the meal. Another person might then bring your meal to you. This can increase the chance that something could become cross-contaminated.

Despite the dangers, thousands of gluten-sensitive people eat out every day. You only need a few restaurants with a gluten-free menu and the ability to ask a few questions.

How to find restaurants that serve gluten- free food

It's easier than ever to find gluten-free restaurants thanks to the internet and smart phones. Restaurants and people are more aware of gluten-free eating now than ever.

You can find gluten-free restaurants by doing some research. You can search the Internet for "gluten-free restaurants in your area" to find all available options.

You can find nearby restaurants using your Smart phone's "Find Me Gluten Free" app.

Referrals are a great way to find gems. Ask trusted friends and family members for recommendations on gluten-free restaurants. Ask your favorite waiter at your local bar for recommendations.

Restaurants don't want customers to leave. They might be willing to work with you to meet your needs. You shouldn't assume that a restaurant offers gluten-free meals. Do your research ahead of time and make sure they have it. It is best to be informed before you arrive hungry or find out that there are no options.

These restaurants currently offer gluten-free meals: Applebee's Bonefish Grill Boston Market California Pizza Kitchen

Carrabba's Italian Grill Chick -fil-A Chipotle Mexican Grill\sIn-N-Out Burger Le Peep Restaurants Noodles & Company Olive Garden\sOn the Border Outback Steakhouse

P.F. Chang's China Bistro Pei Wei Asian Diner\sRed Robin

Uno Chicago Grill

You know what to expect, and you have some options for restaurants, so you are good. Wrong. You can still get gluten if your not careful. It's crucial to inform wait staff immediately if you visit a restaurant that you have dietary restrictions.

What to do When You Get to the Restaurant

Some waitstaff are knowledgeable about gluten-free cooking, while others are more eager to learn and empathetic. Others just don't care. You may have to "educate" your server in order to get what you want.

Instead of leaving the research up to the server, contact the restaurant in advance. Although the hostess might not have all the answers, they may be able to connect you with the manager/assistant manager. This is ideal since they know the chefs and the menu well. If they are not available, call them during off-peak hours to discuss your concerns.

Here are some questions you can ask. Feel free to add questions that relate to your particular needs:

What gluten-free menu items do they have?

What precautions do they take to keep food gluten-free? If they serve pancakes or hamburgers, are the gluten-free ones cooked on the same griddle as the nongluten? Is the salad premixed with croutons or other glutencontaining toppings? Ask if you can be seated with a gluten- knowledgeable member

of the wait staff as some servers are more aware than others.

It is not necessary to check regularly for restaurants that serve gluten-free meals. To ensure that the same procedures for gluten-free dining are being applied, it's a good idea not to do so every six months but to also check on any changes in management.

Even if the restaurant offers a gluten-free menu you need to inform your server so that they can properly handle your order. Your waiter should know that gluten-free food is not allowed. These are the steps you should follow when arriving at your destination:

Ask for the gluten-free menu before being seated. When your server comes to take your drink order, let them know you intend to order from the gluten-free menu. Ask if they can recommend any gluten-free appetizers. This is a great way to alert them that you'll be eating gluten-free throughout the meal.

Ask which salad dressings are gluten-free (don't be surprised if they don't know as this usually isn't a topic of discussion in the kitchen). Places like Amazon.com sells gluten-free salad dressings in portable packets. It's a good idea to keep some in your car or handbag in case a restaurant can't tell you if its dressings are gluten-free.

Confirm that your salad isn't pre-mixed with croutons or any toppings containing gluten. If you have all the answers to your questions, your meal will go smoothly.

Important: If you are dining with others, make sure that you decide where to eat. You'll have plenty of gluten-free options!

Finally, if you feel that something is wrong, don't eat it and don't be afraid of leaving.

What if the CEO of your company asks you to join him for dinner? What if there isn't a gluten- free option? Next, I'll discuss how to handle that.

How to Improvise

Sometimes you will find yourself in a situation where gluten-free food is not available at the restaurant you choose. If you are traveling for work, and your boss asks you to join him or her for dinner, this is an example.

What can you do? There are many options. The obvious option is to decline, unless you don't want to upset your boss. You could also join, but not eat.

You can also improvise. Immediately inform your server of your requirements. Look through the menu to see if there is a gluten-free option. You can cook foods like grilled chicken and side dishes of vegetables in separate pans.

If you don't feel comfortable discussing your dietary preferences with your boss, it is best to speak with the hostess. You can also tell the server your special dietary requirements by pulling them aside.

If you feel comfortable talking to the servers, let them know that you are allergic to gluten. If they aren't sure, ask them to send a chef or manager to check and see what they have to say.

You can also tell them what you like, such as grilled chicken with steamed veggies - all cooked on separate cookware. As long as meat is cooked on a gluten-free, unseasoned surface, it is safe. Fruit and a variety of vegetables can be eaten safely.

You can also order a salad that comes with these instructions: "I would like a salad. Is it available with bread sticks or croutons? I want a salad that doesn't touch any bread."

Ask for olive oil, lemon juice and a splash of vinegar for dressing. You can also use a special vinaigrette (flavoured vinegar and oil) or one of the handy salad dressing packs I mentioned earlier.

It is possible to find safe food. You don't have to do much work, and it may not be exactly what your heart desires.

Summary

It's generally safe to eat at restaurants that offer a gluten - free menu.

You can find restaurants that offer a gluten-free menu by searching on the Internet, or using an app on your Smart phone.

When you find a restaurant with a gluten-free menu, call ahead of time to discuss available options.

When you first arrive at a restaurant, make sure the server knows you need to eat gluten-free. Ask questions to make sure they understand your needs. If they seemed confused or don't know what gluten-free is, talk to the manager or chef. If you're at a restaurant that doesn't offer a gluten-free menu, you can improvise by eating plain salad, fruit orvegetables. Don't forget to ask questions about toppings, bread sticks, etc.

Dining out gives you the opportunity to get out of the house and enjoy food and community, and it provides a respite from cooking and cleaning dishes.

Yes, eating out at restaurants can be more risky than dining at home. Asking questions can help you identify and reduce the risk. You can avoid missing something by having a list of questions ready. I've taken questions about restaurants and waitstaff and placed them on a separate page that you can access from the table. You can find the chapter "Restaurant Questions" at the end.

Chapter 7: Vacationing Gluten-Free

Are you a Grand Canyon visitor? Are you familiar with the Eiffel Tower? Do you long to relax on the beach while sipping a refreshing cocktail?

Are you able to travel, see everything you want, and still be gluten-free?

Your travel dreams can still be realized. You just need to plan and be willing to explore.

How to Plan a Successful Gluten-Free Vacation

Relaxation is the goal of vacations. You don't want your time spent worrying about what to eat or where to eat it. It is not a vacation to go to the supermarket, eat on the couch in your hotel room while you watch TV. You can learn from my mistakes and I have learned from them.

Yes, you can travel gluten-free and still eat it. To make the most of your time away, you will need to create a plan.What are your plans for dinner?

You can now go on vacation because you're gluten-free. You should, however, do some research into what is available at your destination.

The following are the most crucial factors to consider when conducting research:

Where are you going to get gluten-free food? Are there any supermarkets or specialty stores within walking distance? Which restaurants offer gluten-free options?

Is there a kitchen, or at the very least a stove and refrigerator, available?

Sometimes your research pays off, and you can easily book your vacation. However, your research may reveal that planning your vacation is more difficult than you anticipated. Perhaps you haven't been able to find a suitable location that is both affordable and meets your requirements. It's possible that you won't be able to find a single restaurant that serves gluten-free food. Things aren't turning out the way you planned.

It's a good idea to look for another vacation spot if at all possible (I have seen this happen a few times while planning a family vacation). It can be challenging, especially if you have a specific location in mind. But I have a long list of places to visit, and if one doesn't work out, I can easily move on to the next.

How do you know if a location is gluten-free-friendly? The following are the steps I take when planning a trip.

Where Can I Purchase Gluten-Free Food?

Use an Internet browser to look for supermarkets in the area you want to visit. Make your statement as specific as possible. You should consider visiting San Diego, California. Type "San Diego supermarkets" into the search bar. If you want to stay on Coronado Island, you can also type in "Supermarkets Coronado Island."

Notify them of any new grocery stores' location, phone number, and name. Call to see what gluten-free options they have. Check their website for gluten-free options if they have one. You might be able to find the information in a digital version of your local newspaper's circular.

You don't have to be concerned about food safety in supermarkets. Produce, meats, dairy, and beverages are available. It would be beneficial to learn if gluten-free cookies, crackers, and pasta are available.

If you change your search to "organic market" instead of "supermarkets," you can eat organically.

Where can I find gluten-free restaurants?

Substitute "gluten-free Coronado Island" for "supermarkets." This will bring up a list of gluten-free restaurants in the area.

You'll need to write down the phone number and location of any restaurants you're interested in visiting. Other people's experiences at these restaurants may help you decide whether or not to go.

How to Find a Kitchen in a Room

It can be difficult to locate a room with a kitchen. They aren't always available or financially feasible. By eating at home, you'll spend more initially but save money in the long run. With the convenience of a fully equipped kitchen, you can have a stress-free, relaxing vacation.

To find hotels and motels with kitchens, type "Coronado island suites" into your search engine. Many major hotel chains provide affordable suites because they recognize the importance of making guests feel at ease, especially when they are staying for an extended period of time.

You could also rent a condo or a house for a short period of time. Websites like Vacation Rental by Owner (www.vrbo.com) can help you find daily and weekly rates.

What is the purpose of having a kitchen?

When traveling, the most difficult meal to avoid gluten is breakfast. Having a kitchen is fantastic. The majority of hotel continental breakfasts consist of toast, cereal, and pastries. Cross-contamination is a risk when hot foods like bacon and eggs are served buffet-style.

With a kitchen, you can even prepare your own breakfast. After you've finished eating, stop by the cafe for a cup of coffee or tea.

Lunch can be a challenge. Snacking is also available, particularly for children. Having a kitchen makes it easier to keep your children happy, healthy, and gluten-free.

A stove, microwave, and refrigerator should all be included in a kitchen with high-quality appliances. You'll be able to easily bring leftovers from gluten-free restaurants back to your house with these appliances.

Will you have to buy everything from the supermarket to stock your kitchen? What if your favorite gluten-free crackers aren't available at your neighborhood store? Even if you're flying, I've learned that you should bring plenty of gluten-free food with you.

What to Bring

Is it possible to travel with gluten-free foods? You certainly can! My family and I have packed gluten-free food into entire suitcases.

What would you suggest bringing with you? You can store non-perishable, gluten-free foods in sealed containers such as:\sBoxed cereal

Pre-packaged meals such as those offered by Go Picnic Pamela's flour mixture (for making pancakes) (for making pancakes).

Bread Crackers Cookies Soup

Small bags of spices to season your meals (this is a good one!) Protein bars

It will help you save money and be useful if you have to arrive in the middle of the night due to delays.

Get ready to tackle the most difficult part of traveling: finding gluten-free food at airports.

How to Eat Gluten-Free in an Airport\sFinding gluten-free food is the only thing that's more difficult than getting through security at airport security.

Unlike franchises like Chili's and Applebee's, which offer gluten-free meals, very few American airports have restaurants that cater for gluten-free customers. If your flight is delayed, you may end up eating junk food since none of these options are ideal.

A list of gluten-free candy bars that you can buy at the newsstand is a good backup. You can bring packaged food into airport security and through security. However, liquids are not allowed through the airport. You can check with the Transportation Security Administration to see what you are allowed to bring. Most airlines have this information available on their websites.

Traveling can be unpredictable so make sure to pack snacks like crackers, nuts, chips, dried fruit, and nuts. They might be of use to you.

Another option is to bring a gluten-free lunch and eat it at the airport. Check your bags at the airport and then find a seat to eat your lunch.

Check the airport restaurants for gluten-free options if you are on a layover. You can always order a cup of fruit if there isn't something available. Flying can be drying.

Do not forget to visit the ice cream shops. Although it may seem indulgent, it is a better option than eating gluten-free food. Jet lag can be a problem, but having jet lag and an upset stomach is another.

You can find something in the shops and restaurants but not in the grocery store. Grab your list of gluten-free candy bars, and go to the newsstand.

Summary

Find out what grocery stores carry gluten-free food at your destination. Find out what restaurants have gluten-free menus.

Look for a place that has a kitchen close to grocery stores, where you can purchase gluten-free food.

Pack your favorite non-perishable gluten-free food. Avoid airports that may not have gluten-free options.

Bring a pre-prepared meal to eat when you arrive at the airport before going through security. Have a list of chips and candy bars handy so you can buy snacks in the concourse.

You can make traveling less stressful by doing your research ahead of time. You and your family will be happy campers if you make sure that you have everything you need at your destination!

Bon voyage!

Chapter 8: Reading Ingredient Lists

Gluten can sneakily be found in many foods and products. Very few products will tell you that they are gluten-free on the packaging. Most products don't specify whether gluten is an ingredient.

How can you tell if it's in your food, then? It is likely that you will need to do it yourself. It is best to look at the ingredients list on the product. It can be difficult to read ingredients because many foods may contain chemicals or ingredients that you have not heard of.

You can quickly determine if gluten is in a recipe with practice and the right information.

How to Identify Gluten in an Ingredient List

One of the best ways to determine if a product has gluten is by looking at its ingredient list. This section will teach you how to read the ingredient labels. You can determine whether the food is safe or not by looking at its ingredients.

Avoid eating or drinking any food that contains gluten. You can simply return it to the shelf and choose another product. It's that simple!

"If you don't know, don't eat it!"

Gluten is not listed as an ingredient. Therefore, it is important to search for ingredients that contain gluten. It can be difficult to read labels if you don't know all of the ingredients that include gluten.

Good news: You won't have to double-check the ingredients every time you purchase food. Food that is gluten-free today won't necessarily be the same next week. To be certain, I recommend checking the ingredients of any food you eat. Even though it's not a common practice, sometimes ingredients change.

For your convenience, I have added a complete list to the back of the book. This list will help you check for gluten. If you would like a free copy of our Gluten-Free Ingredient List book, simply visit: http://happyglutenfree.com/ingredientreference.

Here are some examples of ingredient labels. I'll show you how to determine if a product has been tested for safety. It may take some time to master how to read labels to determine if the product is gluten-free. But remember, practice makes perfect. You will improve your ability to read ingredients every time you do it.

Labelling Regulations

Federal Nutrition Labeling and Education Act of 1990 requires that all food be labeled with nutrition information and provide details about their content. These labels must include information such as the calories per serving, fat, cholesterol, sodium and fiber. Foods that do not conform to these requirements are deemed misbranded and subject to Food, Drug and Cosmetic Act enforcement provisions.

Further amendments to the FD&CA were made by 2004's Food Allergen Labeling and Consumer Protection Act. The act requires food labels to indicate the presence of eight food allergens. These allergens include milk, eggs and shellfish. These eight allergens account for 90 percent of food allergies. Notice that oats, barley, and rye are not included in the eight-pointed list. Neither are many of wheat's grain cousins, such as semolina or kamut.

All processed and manufactured food labels must contain ingredients. Some products and produce, such as those found at farmer's markets, don't need ingredient labels because they aren't subject to the same food labeling laws. You should always consult the producer or manufacturer

about possible gluten contamination.

Reading a Label

Imagine yourself in a grocery store, and you have just bought a product that interests you. A typical ingredient list is usually found on the back of the package or side of the box. It looks similar to the ones shown in Figures 1 through 4.

Please Note: I have highlighted the ingredients in each image below that could contain gluten or may be gluten-containing.

Figure 1's ingredient label shows that wheat is included. This product should be avoided. Figure 1 shows a cheese and crackers "to-go" product. Prepackaged food with crackers is likely to contain gluten, unless the package or box specifies otherwise.

This is the next example. This candy bar contains barley malt as one of its ingredients. Gluten is found in barley malt, which is an ingredient:

Figure 3's ingredient label is unclear. Although it turned out that the food was gluten-free, the ingredient label in Figure 3 wasn't so clear. I had to contact the manufacturer, who informed me that there were no gluten ingredients:

Vague ingredients like 'Natural' or 'Artificial Flavors' are the most frustrating. Both terms are generalized and can contain gluten. Natural or artificial flavors can come from or contain barley. Many manufacturers I have spoken with note that they will list barley separately as an ingredient if it is used in the flavorings. Nonetheless, I still recommend contacting the manufacturer of any food you are not sure of.

This last ingredient list highlights another important information. Even if the product does not contain gluten, it is important to know the details of the manufacturing facility and equipment:

Figure 4 shows a product label that contains barley malt extract, which is gluten-free. Also, notice the statement at bottom of the label "MADE ON EQUIPMENT ALSO PROCESSES WHEEAT." Another similar statement is "MADE AT A FACILITY ALSO PROCESSES WATER."

Even if the products are not gluten-free, they could be contaminated by gluten if processed in equipment that also processes wheat.

It doesn't matter if the food was made on equipment or in a facility that uses wheat. Talk to the manufacturer for more details. Manufacturers may clean the equipment before making every batch of food. You are most likely safe if the equipment has been cleaned.

If the wheat is processed on the same equipment, but the equipment is not cleaned up properly, there is a high risk of contamination. You should therefore avoid purchasing the product.

Summary

You now know how to determine if a food contains gluten. Refer to the list of unsafe ingredients at the end of the book to verify the foods you are looking at.

It takes practice to become proficient at reading labels. It doesn't matter if it takes a lot of practice at first. It will get easier!

To find out if products contain gluten, do you need to read every label on supermarket shelves? It's not necessary, I've already done a lot of the legwork.

Next, I will discuss safe and gluten-free foods.

Chapter 9: Safe Gluten-Free Foods List

This chapter will cover several safe and gluten-free foods.

It can be confusing and overwhelming to shop for gluten-free food. How can you identify safe foods to eat? I discussed how to read ingredient labels and identify gluten-free foods. It won't take too long, though?

It can take some time to create your own list of gluten-free foods you enjoy and those that are readily available in your local supermarkets. Here are some suggestions to help you get started.

You'll find tips and a list of widely-available gluten-free products that you can buy today.

Gluten-Free Food You Can Buy Today

I have divided gluten-free food into brands and categories that you can buy in most grocery stores. Some of these items may not be available depending on where you live or the size of your community. I also list websites where you could order food online later in this chapter. However, produce such as fruits and vegetables, milk and meat can be found everywhere.

Produce

The produce section allows you to choose any fruits or vegetables that you like. Wheat grass is not recommended in some markets. You can choose from the available options.

Fresh produce is a great way to eat healthy. It is important to note that your body will require more nutrients and water as you remove gluten from your diet. Fresh fruits and vegetables are a great way to provide your body with the nutrients it needs?

Be aware that the dip on pre-made vegetable tray (aka crudites), may not be gluten free. For quick dips, you can grab a vegetable tray and a bottle Newman's Own Ranch dressing. You can also buy fresh vegetables and cut them up. Then, put the dressing in a bowl. Voila! Voila.

Meat

Meat is a great source of iron and protein, which is particularly important when your body is healing. Avoid purchasing pre-marinated meat cuts. Even if the meat isn't gluten-free, marinades from unreliable sources can cause serious damage to your system.

You can make your spice rubs and marinades. All single ingredient spices from McCormick's and Tone's are gluten-free. Mixing different flavors together can be fun.

Many deli meats can be made gluten-free. Be careful when ordering sliced meats or cheeses at the deli counter. Cross contamination of gluten with other products may occur when slicers or counters are used!

Pre-packaged deli meat is safer. These brands may offer gluten-free deli meats, but make sure to check the label:

Hormel Natural Choice Meats Boar's Head\sBuddig Oscar Mayer

Gluten can be used to enhance flavor and texture. Other meat products to look out for include hot dogs, sausages, hot dogs and "loaf" products such as olive loaf.

These brands are safe to eat: Coleman Naturals Hot Dogs

Boulder Sausage (their sausage varieties are labeled glutenfree on the package) (their sausage varieties are labeled glutenfree on the package) Johnsonville Ground Sausage

Smithfield Smoked Sausage Loops Hillshire Farms Smoked Bratwurst Wellshire Farms Original Deli Franks

Ball Park Singles Beef Franks Beer bratwurst contains gluten, so it may seem obvious. Bards is a brand that makes gluten-free beer.

Bread

You will find gluten-free breads in the freezer section along with organic foods. Because there are a small number of people who will eat gluten-free baked goods, they don't sell well. They are also less likely to contain preservatives so it's more cost-effective to freeze them.

If your local supermarket does not carry gluten-free bread, you may need to go to Whole Foods or another natural food store. You can find gluten-free bread at some bakeries, but make sure to ask about crosscontamination. Do they have separate containers and counters for the bread?

Before you buy.

These are the best gluten-free breads:

Rudy's Gluten -Free Bakery

Udi's Gluten Free Bakery Canyon Bakehouse

All three brands can be found in the United States.

Notable: Udi's and Rudy's also make regular breads, so ensure you're buying the gluten-free variety.

Gluten-free bread can be costly so you should expect to pay $5.00 per loaf. You can also find coupons online for the company.

To save money, you can make your own gluten-free bread or use a bread machine. The aroma of freshly baked bread in your home, as well as the delicious homemade flavor, are well worth the extra cost.

Pasta

Pasta is a common household staple. Is it possible to find gluten-free options? Yes!

Gluten-free pasta should be made with brown rice flour. It has a wheat-like flavor and texture. Because gluten-free pasta has more starch than regular pasta, it should be washed immediately after cooking in a colander. Always cook gluten-free pasta until al dente.

It'll become mushy and sticky if you don't.

Gluten-free pasta can be found alongside regular pasta in the natural foods section of the supermarket. Gluten-free areas are now available in a lot of stores. Ask a stock representative if you can't find it. These are the brands that I am most familiar with.

adore:

DeBoles Annie's Homegrown Tinkyada Rice Pasta

Spirals, macaroni, and penne are just a few of the pastas Tinkyada, DeBoles, and DeBoles can make. Tinkyada is also capable of preparing lasagna noodles.

Both Annie's and DeBoles sell gluten-free macaroni and cheese, as well as other gluten-free items.

Wheat pasta is made by DeBoles and Annie's. Make sure you buy gluten-free pasta.

Muffins, cakes, cookies, muffins, and pancakes are best enjoyed when baked with flour. It's more difficult to bake with gluten-free flour than with regular flour. Some foods, however, are more difficult to bake than others. If you have the right flour, you can make gluten-free pancakes.

On the market, there are numerous gluten-free flours. Each flour is made up of a different gluten-free grain flour blend. They're the most common ingredients in gluten-free flour mixtures, along with tapioca starch, white rice flour, and sorghum flour.

Gluten-free flour mixtures are not easy to substitute for wheat flour, despite what their labels claim. They have distinct flavors and textures when added to food. It can be challenging to replace wheat flour in a recipe if you're new to gluten-free flour. There are a few exceptions that are delectable and delectable.

The best results come from recipes that can be made gluten-free. You're encouraged to try new things and see what works best for you.

These are the best gluten-free flours to buy pre-made and how to use them. These flour blends are readily available both online and in stores:

Pamela's Gluten-Free Pancake Mix is a delicious gluten-free pancake mix from Pamela's Kitchen (pancakes, crepes, cookies) Gluten-Free Flour, Bob's Red Mill (easiest to find, best for cookies)

Gluten-Free Bisquick Flour (Bisquick) (great for muffins)

Gluten-Free Cake Mix Betty Crocker (chocolate, vanilla) Gluten-Free Brownie Mix from Betty Crocker

One of my favorite pancake mixes is Pamela's. Betty Crocker cake mixes are included in the Betty Crocker mix package. On the boxes, it says "gluten-free."At your local grocery store, you may find several gluten-free flours in individual packages. These flours are most commonly found at Bob's Red Mill, but they can also be found at other brands. To make your own flour mixtures, you'll need these flours. Carol Fenster and Bette Hagman, two well-known gluten-free chefs, have developed flour blends that can be used to make a variety of breads and cakes.

Dairy

If you can tolerate milk products, many dairy products are gluten-free. Lactose intolerance is common among celiac disease patients who have recently been diagnosed. They must refrain from eating dairy products until they have fully recovered.

If you can tolerate dairy, these foods are safe to eat: Eggs

Eggs (if using Ener-G powder or Egg Beaters instead of eggs, make sure it's gluten-free)

Milk

All types of milk, including half-and-half, whipping cream, skim, 1 percent, 2 percent, and whole milk, are safe to consume. Not all flavored or nondairy milks, however, are gluten-free. As a result, it's best to double-check the ingredients before making a purchase.

Some milks are gluten-free, such as:

Nesquik comes in a variety of ready-to-drink flavors. Coffee-mate comes in a variety of flavors.

Horizon is available in a variety of flavors, including chocolate and strawberry. Soy Milk and Organic Valley Eggnog (vanilla)

Buttermilk

Almond, hazelnut, rice, and soy milk cheese from Pacific Natural Foods

Is it true that cheese is gluten-free? The majority of it is, but not all of it. Blocks of cheddar, Monterey Jack, and Swiss cheese, for example, are safe. It's fine to use pre-shredded Kraft mozzarella, cheddar, or Parmesan. Other cheeses that are safe to eat include:

Laughing Cow Babybel and Wedges from Kraft Singles Athenos cheeses Frigo Ricottas

shredded and sliced Sargento varieties Regular Velveeta

Tillamook cheeses are made in Oregon.

Yogurt and sour cream

Sour cream and yogurt are two dairy products you'll almost certainly have on hand. Here are a few national gluten-free brands:

Sour Cream Daisy

Stonyfield Fat Free, Low Fat, and Whole Milk Yogurt Knudsen Sour Cream and Yogurt Sour Cream and Yogurt from Tillamook On the package, Yoplait yogurts state whether or not they are gluten-free.

Cereal

It's convenient to keep a few boxes of cereal on hand for a quick breakfast or snack:

Chocolate, Cinnamon, Corn, Honey Nut, and Rice Chex Eco-Planet Original Instant Hot Cereal Nature's Path by General Mills Koala Crisp or Amazon Frosted Flakes

Don't assume that all Chex cereal from General Mills is gluten-free. On the front of the box, look for the words "gluten-free." Nature's Path gluten-free cereals are tasty, and they have several varieties that are suitable for children.

Sauces for Pasta

Pasta sauce is obviously delicious when served with pasta. However, marinara can also be used as a pizza sauce or a dip for gluten-free bread sticks. For years, I've used Newman's Own Marinara as a pizza sauce and dip.

Unfortunately, not all gluten-free pasta sauces are available. However, these sauces are currently: Classico red and white sauces from Dei Fratelli Newman's Own (Newman's Own)

Dressings for Salad

Salad dressing, like pasta sauce, can be used for more than just salad. It can also be used as a marinade or a dip. Here's a list of gluten-free salad dressings:

Cookwell & Company Cracked Black Pepper Vinaigrette Bolthouse Farms Newman's Own Ranch, Balsamic Vinaigrette, and Caesar Kraft Thousand Island and Ranch

Salad dressings aren't all gluten-free. So read the ingredients (you're probably getting pretty good at it by now!) and double-check with the manufacturer to see what's safe and what's not.

Summary

Gluten-free foods include a variety of foods that you may be familiar with. Furthermore, meat, produce, and many dairy products are all safe to eat and are widely available.

Some items are more specialized and difficult to come by. In that case, I recommend going to one of these websites to look for the products: Amazon.com: With an Amazon Prime membership, you also get free two-day shipping and low-cost overnight shipping.

Celiac.com - The Gluten-Free Mall: Celiac.com is one of the first online gluten-free grocery stores.

There are numerous gluten-free food options available to you. However, you should be aware of foods to avoid. I'll go over them in the next chapter.

Foods to Avoid (Chapter 10)

By now, you've probably realized that eating gluten-free is very feasible. Many of the brands listed above are likely familiar to you, and you may have even used them before.

While the food I mentioned earlier is safe, what about food that isn't? Every grocery store has three types of food: safe, unsafe, and those you're not sure about.

Gluten can be found in a variety of places, as I previously stated. You will be aware of which foods contain gluten if you know what foods to avoid. Why should you know what foods are dangerous?

Gluten is clearly present in some products, such as Wheaties. Others, on the other hand, are less obvious. Take, for example, soy sauce (which is made from fermented wheat). Play-Doh, for example, is a wheat-based product. It's important to know which foods are safe, but it's also important to know which foods to avoid when following a gluten-free diet.

When eating gluten-free, stay away from the following foods.

Wheat, barley, and rye are the most common gluten-containing grains. However, did you know that there are a number of wheat and barley-related grains you should avoid as well?

Kamut Club Durum Spelt Bulgur Einkorn Semolina Bulgur Einkorn Semolina Bulgur Einkorn Semol

Graham

Several types of unused glutenfree flour were offered to me by a friend of a friend. They had tried going gluten-free because they were experiencing similar symptoms. Gluten-free eating had not helped them for some reason. So they were trying to get rid of these flours, and I offered to take them. They gave us semolina flour in one of the bags (which is not gluten-free). Yikes!

It's no surprise they weren't improving because they hadn't completely eliminated gluten from their diet! This is unfortunate because they never allowed their bodies to fully heal as a result of eating a gluten-free diet.

What Foods Contain Gluten?

You must completely eliminate gluten from your diet to feel your best and become symptom-free, which, of course, means eliminating gluten-containing foods.

So, what are some of the most common gluten-containing foods? Pasta Crusts Made of Bread Muffins Cookies Cupcakes Cake Croutons

Tortillas made of flour Tarts

Buns Bagels Cereal Donuts Green chili Gravy Pudding Breading Bullion Soup Malted milkshake Pizza

Nutrition bars

Fried food (including French fries) (including French fries) Enchilada, Hoisin and teriyaki sauces

These basic food items make up hundreds of the most popular meals in today's culture. No wonder going gluten-free can be so hard at first! Were you surprised by any of the ingredients on that list? I myself was shocked to learn about all the places where gluten hides.

Where Else Does Gluten Hide?

I talked earlier about the characteristics of gluten that make it so useful. Following are other non- food products that may contain gluten, such as: Shampoo\sConditioner Cosmetics Lipstick Makeup Lip balm Sun block Medicine Play-Doh

Kid's paints

If you have children note that Play-Doh is made with wheat flour, so it is one to watch out for because kids like to eat it! The Kaplan Early Learning Company offers a gluten-free alternative to Play-Doh for sale on Amazon.com. I have included a recipe to make your own version in the "Recipes" which is located at the back of this book.

Summary

Some surprising foods and products contain gluten. By understanding what those foods and products are, you know what foods to stay away from.

Now that you know about food that is glutenfree and safe and food that's unsafe, you might be wondering how you can you eat gluten-free without blowing your food budget. My next chapter, "Be Thrifty," gives tips on how to eat healthy while saving money.

Chapter 11: Eating Gluten-Free on a Budget

It is a fact that eating gluten-free is expensive. So how do you keep costs low and your spirits high? The key is to focus your budget on inexpensive food that does the best job of satisfying your family's hunger and your dietary needs.

The food industry has people hooked on eating cheap, easily accessible, throwaway products. Ever witness how fast a bag of Oreo's cookies disappears from the pantry? You might not know it yet, but the gluten-free equivalent of Oreo's costs almost double (did you hear your wallet scream?).

You don't have money to waste. So why spend it on sugary gluten-free food that provides little to no nutritional value?

Why is Gluten-Free Food More Expensive?

Before going gluten-free you were probably used to buying bread and cookies at reasonably low prices. But now that you are on a new diet, glutenfree equivalents are produced in smaller batches. And the ingredients to make those equivalents – like gluten-free flour — are more expensive.

Additionally, some gluten-free food manufacturers use special tests to certify that they comply with gluten-free requirements — an expense that ultimately gets passed on to you. It's simple economics that higher production costs result in higher food prices. Hopefully, as more people eat gluten-free, more gluten-free food will be produced and the cost will come down.

What Gluten-Free Food is the Most Expensive?

The most expensive gluten-free foods are those that use specialty glutenfree ingredients. For example, a small bag half-pound bag of glutenfree brown rice flour, which is a common ingredient in baked goods, costs about the same as a two pound bag of wheat flour.

What does that tell you? If that bag of brown rice flour is expensive for you, it is expensive for the manufacturer too.

It makes sense then, that the most expensive gluten-free foods are baked goods that use expensive ingredients. Foods like cookies, cakes, cupcakes, breads, muffins, and nutrition bars are the most expensive.

You might say, "Well, it's baked in a dedicated gluten-free facility. And that's supposed to be a good thing." Well, yes it is. But you're paying extra for that manufacturing safety. There are healthy gluten-free food items that cost the same no matter what diet you're on. As a result, you must seek for those that are both healthy and economical.

Which gluten-free foods are the most affordable?

Produce. Fruits and vegetables are gluten-free by nature, and they fulfill both hunger and nutritional requirements.

Meat, as long as it isn't pre-seasoned, pre-marinated, or packed with taste enhancers. Several simple dairy products are available.

Nuts are gluten-free in a lot of chips and crackers.

To make sure they're gluten-free, none of them need any extra ingredients or processing. It's just how they're wired.

You may believe that getting your family to eat fruits and veggies is impossible. You also can't imagine life without sandwiches and buns (remember the gluten-free alternatives I mentioned previously).

Keeping everyone pleased at meals is a difficult task. You do, however, have a limited budget for food. So, on a low budget, what can you serve?

How to Minimize Spending

If you're on a budget, feeding your family nutritious, wholesome meals should be your first priority.

Staples

Fruits, vegetables, nuts, and meat provide the most protein and nutritious value. Salad is a delicious meal in and of itself or as a side dish to any meal. Dairy comes in second place in terms of cost efficiency: eggs and cheese are just as significant as milk (dried milk is less costly than fresh).

Cereal is the next most important food (again, some General Mills Chex cereals are glutenfree). Because they're supplemented with vitamins and minerals, they're the most cost-effective and nutritious option.

Pasta and bread without gluten. Gluten-free buns might be expensive, so avoid purchasing them. It won't take long for your family to get accustomed to eating hot dogs and hamburgers without them, saving you a lot of money each year.

Snacks

Gluten-free potato or corn chips come in huge, affordable packs. Nuts are pricey, but they fill you up quickly, requiring you to eat fewer calories.

Costco and Sam's Club both sell large packs of gluten-free Crunchmaster MultiGrain Crackers.

Beverages

Instead of sodas or bottled juice, use frozen concentrates if your family like sweet drinks.

It's possible you've noticed that I've left out cookies, muffins, and ice cream. It's fantastic if you have any money left over for such luxuries. If you're on a budget, though, concentrate on foods that will keep you and your wallet alive!

Gluten-free food is more costly since it is more difficult to produce.

The most costly gluten-free items include gluten-free bread, cupcakes, cakes, muffins, and cookies. Produce, meat, basic dairy, and chips are all cheaper.

Purchasing protein-rich, nutrient-dense foods can keep your family well-fed while also keeping your budget in control.

Gluten-free eating is a delicate balancing act between deliciousness and affordability. It might seem like a hardship to give up cookies, cakes, and muffins since they are so delicious.

However, you must maintain your family healthy, therefore prioritize protein-dense, high-nutrient gluten-free foods like meat, fruits, and vegetables in your budget.

Conclusion

Gluten-Free for Beginners was written with the main objective of assisting you in overcoming the challenges of becoming gluten-free. Making a change like this to your diet requires a lot of dedication, but I admire you for doing so.

Following this book's research...

You've got everything you need to live a gluten-free, healthy life. You're well aware of what gluten is and how it may harm you and your loved ones.

You now know how to keep your house gluten-free in a safe manner, which should make you very happy. Cross-contamination is just too important to be overlooked, as you have discovered. You'll be less likely to ingest gluten by mistake now that you're aware of it.

You know what procedures to take while traveling or eating out to get a healthy gluten-free meal. You now know how to create a gluten-free diet plan and explain your requirements to anyone who come into touch with your food, such as family members and wait staff.

You've discovered that not all gluten-free foods are clearly labeled, but that doesn't mean you can't consume them. You can figure out if it's safe to eat with a little study.

Request from a Friend

I hope you enjoyed this book and learned something useful from it.

I value positive feedback from people like you. Would you mind writing a review if you found it helpful?

Please let me know if I need to make any changes to this book. Please let me know if you find any errors or have any suggestions so that I can improve the book.

Producing high-quality goods is important to me. So, if you notice anything I've missed, please let me know.

Please contact me at jim@happyglutenfree.com with any suggestions. This email will be sent to me directly, rather than through an assistant or other intermediary.

Please accept my sincere gratitude in advance for your feedback.

Additional Literature Shirley, James L

Other useful books can be found here. A Shopping Guide for Gluten-Free Meals Taco Recipes: 10 Delicious Options

Concerns about eating places

Here are some good questions to ask (feel free to add any that pertain to your special needs):

1. Do they have any gluten-free menu items?

2. What gluten-free precautions do they take?

3. Are gluten-free pancakes or hamburgers prepared on the same griddle as regular pancakes or hamburgers?

4. Are croutons or other gluten-containing toppings pre-mixed in the salad?

5. Request to be seated with a member of the wait staff who is gluten-aware, as some servers are more knowledgeable than others.

Remember that finding out which restaurants serve gluten-free food is something you should do on a regular basis. It's a good idea to check in every six months or so to see what changes have occurred, as well as any time management changes, to ensure that the same gluten-free dining protocols are being followed.

Even if you are aware that the restaurant offers a gluten-free menu, you should speak with your server when you arrive to ensure that your order is handled correctly. Always inform your waiter or waitress that you require gluten-free cuisine. Following is a list of things to do when you get there:

1. Before taking a seat, ask for the gluten-free menu.

2. Inform your server that you will be ordering from the gluten-free menu when your drink order is taken.

3. Inquire if any gluten-free appetizers are available. This is an excellent way to inform them that you will be gluten-free for the duration of the meal.

4. Inquire about gluten-free salad dressings (don't be surprised if they don't know; this isn't something that comes up in the kitchen very often). Gluten-free salad dressings in packets are available on sites like Amazon.com. If a restaurant can't tell you if its dressings are gluten-free, keep some in your car or handbag.

5. Double-check that your salad doesn't include gluten-containing croutons or toppings.

If all of your questions have been satisfactorily answered, your meal should be successful.

Recipes

Recipes for fun dough, breakfast, lunch, and dinner can be found on the following pages. The menu suggestions from earlier in the book are complemented by these recipes.

Kids Fun Dough Recipe

Make your own Play-Doh type dough. (Recipe from Parents Magazine) 1/2 cup rice flour

1/2 cup corn starch 1/2 cup salt

2 teaspoons cream of tartar (that'll keep the kids from eating it!) 1 cup water 1 teaspoon cooking oil

Mix the ingredients. At this point, you can add food coloring for fun. Cook and stir on low heat for 3 minutes or until a ball is formed. Cool completely and then store in a seal-able plastic bag.

Breakfast Menu Recipes

Berry Smoothie

1 cup fresh or frozen berries, any kind 1/2 cup apple juice

1/2 cup milk 1/4 cup yogurt

1/2 teaspoon vanilla

Combine all the ingredients in a mixer and blend until smooth. Makes two servings.

Breakfast Pancakes

1 cup Pamela's Pancake Mix 3/4 cup milk or water

1 tablespoon olive oil 1/4 teaspoon vanilla 1 large egg

Mix the milk, egg, oil, and vanilla together well. Add the Pamela's mix in and stir until a lumpy batter forms. Cook the pancakes on a griddle at 325 degrees Fahrenheit. Makes four servings.

Breakfast Tacos

1 tablespoon butter

5 ounces chorizo (about 1/3 of a pound) 1/2 medium white onion, diced

1 jalapeño pepper, diced 5 large eggs Also:

8 - 12 corn tortillas grated Monterey Jack cheese pico de gallo

1/4 teaspoon chili powder (optional)

Warm corn tortillas in aluminum foil at 300 degrees for 15 minutes. Whisk the eggs in a medium bowl and set aside. Melt the butter in a large skillet over medium heat. Add the chorizo and break it into small chunks. Fry until the chorizo is browned and the fat has mostly cooked away. Add the onion and pepper. Let cook about two minutes before adding the egg. Mix with a spatula until the eggs are scrambled. Lightly sprinkle chili powder on the mixture for a spicy kick.

Remove the corn tortillas and stack two per taco on each plate. Spoon the chorizo egg mixture on each taco, cover with cheese, and garnish with pico de gallo.

Cheese Omelette

Non-stick cooking spray or 1 teaspoon butter 2 eggs

1/2 teaspoon salt 1/2 teaspoon black pepper 1/4 teaspoon dill

1/8 cup gluten-free, shredded cheddar cheese

Heat a small non-stick skillet over medium heat. Spray the skillet with the cooking spray or melt the butter.

In a small bowl, whisk the eggs and seasonings together. Pour the egg mixture into the skillet. Cook over medium heat, swirling the pan occasionally to ensure the eggs uniformly cover the bottom of the pan. Flip the omelet when it is almost set. Cook an additional 30 seconds. Sprinkle the cheese over one side, fold the omelet and slide it onto a plate. Makes one serving.

Lunch Menu Recipes

3 Cheese Pasta Bake

1 pound gluten-free penne 2 cups heavy cream

1 (14-ounce) can crushed tomatoes 2 cup bag shredded Italian cheese 1/2 teaspoon salt

1/2 teaspoon black pepper 1/2 teaspoon nutmeg

1/2 cup chopped fresh basil

Prepare the pasta according to package directions. Rinse and drain.

Preheat the oven to 400 degrees Fahrenheit. In a large bowl, combine the remaining ingredients. Stir in the pasta. Pour this mixture into a 9 by 13 inch pan. Bake for 20 minutes, or until the top is browned. Makes six servings.

Asian Coleslaw Dressing:

1/4 cup gluten-free Tamari soy sauce juice and zest of one lime 1 teaspoon sugar 1/2 teaspoon salt 1/2 teaspoon black pepper 1/2 teaspoon ginger

1/2 teaspoon cayenne pepper 1/2 teaspoon minced garlic 1/2 cup vegetable oil

Salad:

2 cups cabbage, sliced thinly 1/2 cup chopped red pepper 2 carrots, grated 2 green onions, chopped 1/4 cup cilantro, chopped 1/4 cup chopped peanuts

Combine the dressing ingredients and refrigerate for up to four hours. Toss the dressing with the salad ingredients and refrigerate or serve immediately. Makes six servings.

Broccoli Cheese Soup

1/2 pound broccoli, washed and cut in 2 inch pieces 2 cups milk

2 tablespoons cornstarch

1 cup shredded cheddar cheese 1/2 teaspoon salt

1/2 teaspoon onion powder 1/2 teaspoon black pepper 1/2 teaspoon nutmeg

Steam or boil the broccoli until tender. Puree in a food processor or blender. Combine the broccoli with the milk and cornstarch and heat over medium heat, stirring frequently, until the mixture begins to thicken. Add the remaining ingredients and cook an additional 5 minutes, or until the cheese melts. Makes six servings.

Chicken and Spinach Salad Dressing:

1/4 cup vinegar

1 tablespoon orange juice concentrate 1/2 teaspoon dry mustard powder

1/2 teaspoon salt 1/2 teaspoon black pepper 1 teaspoon honey

1/2 cup vegetable oil Salad:

2 cups washed spinach 1/2 cup shredded chicken 1/2 cup chopped pecans 1 avocado, diced

1/2 cup gluten-free feta cheese

1 (8 ounce) can mandarin oranges, drained

Toss the salad ingredients in a large bowl. In a smaller bowl, combine the vinegar, orange juice, honey and seasonings. Slowly add the oil, whisking for 30 seconds, or until smooth. Refrigerate the dressing for at least one hour prior to serving for best flavor. Makes six servings.

Strawberry Salad Dressing:

1/4 cup red wine vinegar 1/2 teaspoon dry mustard 1/2 teaspoon salt 1/2 teaspoon black pepper

2 tablespoons gluten-free strawberry jam 1 tablespoon diced onion

1/2 cup vegetable oil Salad: 2 cups spinach or baby greens 1/2 cup sliced strawberries 1/2 cup slivered almonds

1/4 cup shelled edamame 1/4 cup diced red bell pepper

1/4 cup crumbed, gluten-free bacon

Combine all the dressing ingredients in a blender. Whirl for 30 seconds, or until thick and completely combined. Refrigerate for at least two hours to blend flavors. Toss with salad ingredients and serve immediately. Makes six servings.

Tomato Basil Pasta

2 Roma tomatoes, diced

1/2 cup fresh mozzarella, cut in 1 inch cubes 1/2 cup fresh, chopped basil

1/2 cup olive oil 1/2 teaspoon salt

1/2 teaspoon black pepper 1/2 teaspoon minced garlic

1 pound gluten-free penne pasta

Combine all the ingredients except the pasta in a large serving dish. Allow it to sit for 30 minutes to allow the flavors to meld. Boil the pasta according to package directions, rinse and drain. Toss the pasta with the tomato mixture and serve. Makes six servings.

Dinner Menu Recipes Beef Burgundy

2 strips gluten-free bacon 1/2 cup diced onion 1/2 cup chopped mushrooms

1 pound stew meat or pot roast, cut in 2 inch cubes 1 cup red wine

1 cup gluten-free beef broth

2 tablespoons tapioca flour

2 tablespoons tomato paste

1/2 teaspoon salt

1/2 teaspoon black pepper 1/2 teaspoon minced garlic 1/2 teaspoon thyme

Cook the bacon in a large skillet until crispy and browned. Drain on paper towels and crumble. Add the onions and mushrooms to the bacon drippings and cook until tender, stirring frequently, 3 to 4 minutes. Place in the slow cooker. Brown the beef in the bacon drippings, until browned on all sides. Transfer to the slow cooker. Add the remaining ingredients, including the bacon, and cook on low 6 hours. Serve with mashed potatoes or gluten-free noodles. Makes six servings.

Note: Cornstarch is often used as a thickening agent in gluten-free cooking, but it breaks down with extended heat. Tapioca flour works better in the slow cooker. Makes six servings.

Chicken Cacciatore

2 tablespoons vegetable oil

4 boneless, skinless chicken breasts 1 onion, cut in rings 1 green bell pepper, cut in rings 1/2 cup mushrooms, sliced 1 clove garlic, minced 1 (14.5 ounce) can diced tomatoes, drained 1 (6 ounce) can tomato paste

1 cup water

1 teaspoon salt

1/2 teaspoon black pepper 1 teaspoon dried basil

1/2 teaspoon dried oregano

Heat the oil in a large skillet. Add the chicken breasts and sauté for 10 minutes, or until browned.

Add the onions, peppers, and mushrooms and cook an additional 5 minutes. Stir in the remaining ingredients. Cover and simmer for 30 minutes. Makes six servings.

Chicken Enchiladas

1 tablespoon vegetable oil 1/4 cup minced onion 1 clove garlic, minced 1 (6 ounce) can diced green chiles 2 cups shredded chicken

1/2 teaspoon salt

1/2 teaspoon black pepper

1/2 teaspoon chipotle chili powder 1/2 teaspoon cumin

8 gluten-free corn tortillas

1/2 cup shredded cheddar or Mexican cheese Enchilada Sauce:

2 cups gluten-free chicken broth 3 tablespoons chili powder

1/2 teaspoon garlic powder 1/2 teaspoon ground cumin

1/2 teaspoon chipotle chili powder 2 tablespoons cornstarch

Preheat the oven to 350 degrees Fahrenheit. To make the enchilada sauce, combine all the ingredients in a medium saucepan. Heat over medium high heat until the sauce boils and thickens, stirring frequently.

Heat the oil in a medium skillet. Add the onion and garlic and cook until tender. Add the remaining ingredients, except the corn tortillas and cheese and heat for 5 minutes, stirring to mix. Place the tortillas in a 9 by 13 inch baking dish and heat in the oven for 5 minutes to soften them. (cont'd)

To fill the tortillas, dip them in the enchilada sauce, lay them in the pan and fill each with ½ cup of the chicken and onion filling. Roll them up and place them, seam side down, in the pan. Top with the remaining enchilada sauce and the cheese. Bake for 30 minutes, or until bubbly. Makes six servings.

Grilled Salmon

3 tablespoons gluten-free Tamari soy sauce juice and zest of one lemon 1 teaspoon minced garlic

1/2 teaspoon black pepper 1/2 teaspoon salt 4 salmon fillets

Combine the Tamari soy sauce, lemon juice and seasonings in a shallow dish or plastic bag. Place the salmon in the bag carefully and marinate for six hours or overnight. Drain. Heat the grill to medium high. Brush the grill grates with oil to prevent sticking. Grill the salmon 6 minutes on each side. Makes four servings.

Ground Beef Tacos

1 pound lean ground beef 1 cup red salsa

1 tablespoon garlic, minced (about 2 medium cloves) 1 1/2 teaspoons chili powder

1/2 teaspoon dried oregano

1/8 teaspoon cayenne pepper (optional) Also:

8 - 12 taco shells grated cheddar or Monterey Jack cheese shredded romaine lettuce 1 chopped tomato sour cream salsa

Place a rack in the middle of the oven and warm to 170 degrees. Sprinkle grated cheddar cheese in the taco shells before you put them in the oven. The melted cheese keeps the taco shells from breaking so easily.

In a large skillet, warm the salsa and garlic over medium heat. Add the ground beef and break it up until it is crumbly. Cook until the meat is browned, about 12 minutes. If there is still grease in the pan, drain it off to avoid greasy tacos. Add the chili powder, oregano, and cayenne (if you use it) and mix well.

Spoon the meat into taco shells and serve. Have lettuce, cheese, sour cream, tomato, and salsa ready for garnishing.

Meatloaf

1 tablespoon vegetable oil 1/2 cup chopped onion 1/2 cup chopped red bell pepper 1/2 cup gluten-free bacon crumbles 1 pound lean ground beef

1 cup gluten-free oatmeal 1 egg, beaten

1 teaspoon salt

1/2 teaspoon black pepper 1/2 teaspoon thyme

3 tablespoons gluten-free ketchup 1 teaspoon dry mustard powder 1/2 teaspoon brown sugar

Preheat the oven to 350 degrees Fahrenheit. Heat the oil in a medium skillet. Add the onion and bell pepper and cook until tender. Combine the onion, pepper, bacon, ground beef, oatmeal, egg and seasonings in a large bowl. Mix thoroughly and place in a loaf pan or 8 inch baking dish.

Combine the ketchup, mustard and brown sugar in a small bowl. Pour over the ground beef and smooth with a spoon. Bake for 45 minutes, or until the meatloaf is fully cooked. Makes four servings.

Teriyaki Chicken

4 boneless skinless chicken breasts 1/4 cup gluten-free teriyaki sauce 1/2 teaspoon minced garlic

1 tablespoon honey juice and zest of one orange

Place the chicken breasts in a slow cooker. Stir together the remaining ingredients and pour over the chicken. Cook on low for 4 to 6 hours, turning the chicken halfway through. Makes four servings.

CPSIA information can be obtained
at www.ICGtesting.com
Printed in the USA
LVHW021358280122
709444LV00011B/594